Independent
Compact Cars

Hudson-Kaiser-Nash-Studebaker-Willys

Hudson Jet Factory press kit photo

By Don Narus

www.newalbanybooks.com

ICC11919

Contents

Printed and published in the United States of America by LuLu Press, Inc. Morrisville,NC 27560. Distributed by New Albany Books, Palm Harbor,FL 34684

ACKNOWLEDGEMENTS
and PHOTO CREDITS

The images reproduced in this book are digital, direct download digital jpg images of various sizes. Some are originally black and white (usually Factory or Archived Photos). Others are color photo / images converted to black and white using a greyscale process. While all images were necessary to the content of this book their quality varies. The best images available at the time, for the examples shown, were chosen. Every attempt was made to provide the best image. We also realize that photos are subjective. If better images or a conversion process becomes available after the initial publication, they will be used in later revised editions. Any infringement of copyright photos is unintentional.

Every attempt was made to give credit to each photo used in this book, if we missed someone I apologize, it was not intentional. Know that every photo is important to the content of this book. Thank you all and especially to the following; Auto-Lit.com, coceptcarz.com, HymanLtd.com, Barrett-Jackson.com, momentcars.com, Mecumauctions.com, wikipedia.com, flickr.com, flickrriver.com, Curbsideclassics.com, DanielSchmittandCompany.com, HowstuffWorks.com, carsonline.com, vilocity.com, findclassiccars.com, wheelsage.org, membrs.chello.com, oldcaradvertising.com, ebay.com, motoexotica.com, ateupwithmotor.com, momentcar.com, supercars.com, hiverminer.com, wallpaperup.com, collectorcarads.com, studebakerskytop.com, francislombardi.nl, vintageadbrowser.com, curbsideclassics.com, streetsideclassics.com, barnfinds.com, route66hotrodhigh.com, pinterest.com, classiccardb.com, autowp.ru, hibid.com,americancars-for-sale.com, motor-car.net, topclassicsforsale.com, ebay.com, oldcaradvertising.com,en.wheelsage.org, car-from-uk.com, motorlandamerica.com, automobilesoftheworld.com, diecast.org, carcabin.com, curbsideclassics.com, dailturismo.com, smclassics.com, chromejewlen.com, findclassiccars.com, gomotors.net, studebakerresource.com, internettrader.com, oldcaradvertising.com city-data.com, bringatrailer.com, howstuffworks.com, HenryJcars.com,Mr.Fifty, motorlandamerica.com oldcarsonline.com,davidclassiccars.com, classicvehicleslist.com, collectorcarads.com, american-automobiles.com, carstyleceritic.blogspot.com, automotivereport.com, youtube,com, willinet.com, carsonline-ads.com, classicmotorcarauctions.com, volocars.com, chrisdenove.ebay, classiccars.com, volomuseum-Volo,Ill.

Front Cover: Photo from en.wheelsage.org

Back Cover: Photo from curbsideclassics.com

Introduction

In Post-World War II American auto makers, for the most part, had no reason for any major changes, there was no shortage of customers clamoring for new cars. There were waiting lists for warmed over 1942 designed cars. This continued from 1946 through 1948 (with the exception of Kaiser-Frazer, who began building cars in 1946 and Studebaker who introduced an all new car in 1947. Tucker, Hudson, Oldsmobile and Cadillac introduced all new models in 1948). A new car, was a new car, even if it looked like a 1942 model.

The big changes came in 1949 when all the manufacturers adopted slab sided designs. Competition was fierce. Auto makers were in a fight for customers. It was during this time that George Mason President of Nash Motors division of Nash-Kelvinator and one of the leading Independent auto makers, decided to take a huge gamble. He realized that going head to head with the big three may prove to be fatal to a smaller company such as Nash. A new approach was needed.

Mason's idea was to create a smaller version of its larger cars, with its new unibody construction. Something more "compact". Thus the Nash Rambler was born, The new compact was introduced on April 13, 1950. The initial offering was a 2-door convertible referred to as a "Landau". This single model was followed by a hardtop, sedan, station wagon and sedan delivery, all 2-door models. The first year production for the single model convertible was 9,330 units.

Nash was joined by Kaiser-Frazer, a new auto maker debuting in 1947, who also unveiled their compact, the Henry J. in 1951. Others soon followed: Willys in 1952, Hudson in 1953, with their compact models. Studebaker got into the market in 1963, following Ford, Chevrolet and Chrysler who released their compacts in 1962. But it was the Independents who led the way in creating a new category of car referred to, as the "Compact Car" *, eventually all auto makers world wide, would be producing a compact car.

In this book we cover the independent auto makers in alphabetical order not in the chronological order in which their compacts were introduced.

Don Narus

*The term "Compact Car" would become interchangeable with "Intermediate". Eventually another segment called the "Sub-Compact" would also be used to describe a Micro Car smaller than a "Compact"

Independent
Compact Cars
Hudson-Kaiser-Nash-Studebaker-Willys

By Don Narus

Copyright 2019
ISBN 978-0-359-50003-1

Published by
LuLu Press, Inc. Morrisville, NC

Distributed by
New Albany Books, Palm Harbor, FL

First Edition

Narus, Donald J. (Don)
    1. Compact cars, 2.Independent auto makers, 3.Hudson, 4.Kaiser, 5.Nash
        6. Studebaker, 7. Willys

www.newalbanybooks.com

NEW <u>kind</u> of car in the lowest price field

ECONOMICAL as a Scot

COMPACT, a delight to handle, drive and park

Exquisite as a jewel case...quick and powerful as a panther

HUDSON *JET*

Because it's wonderfully compact, it's a delight to handle, drive and park in today's traffic . . . and there's ample room for six.

Nothing you've ever driven could prepare you for the thrill of your first ride in the Jet. For nothing like it has ever been built before . . . *couldn't be* if it weren't for exclusive "step-down" design that enables it to handle more power for its weight than has ever been put in a car in this field.

This is the answer to traffic and jammed streets . . . a perfect jewel of a car that a woman can park in a tight place or back out of a narrow garage. One ride tells you it's a performer—one look that it's luxuriously beautiful; that it has quality in every detail. Try the Hudson Jet at your dealer's.

Standard trim and color specifications and accessories subject to change without notice.

In durability and quality a worthy companion to the HUDSON HORNET AND HUDSON WASP

Hudson Jet
1953-1954

Because of limited cash flow, Hudson got into the compact car market three years after the Nash Rambler debuted. When it became evident they could no longer ignore the growing interest of this new kind of car, Hudson jumped in with both feet. Choosing the design of the new car presented a challenge, and a good amount of turmoil. First, Hudson President A.E. Barit, like Chrysler's President Keller, was old school and insisted on a high roof line, so drivers and passengers could wear their hats while traveling. He also insisted on chair high seating. The companies stylists wanted a lower, wider, sleeker car. Barit also wanted high rear fenders and round tail lights, like the Oldsmobile. To further complicate matters, Brait enlisted the input of Jim Moran, Hudson's largest dealer. Moran liked the wrap around window. styling of the 1952 Ford. So that had to be incorporated into the overall design. In the end the Compact Hudson Jet, resembled a scaled down version of the 1952-53 Ford Crestline.

The unitized Jet body was produced by Murray Corporation of Detroit who agreed to amortize the tooling costs over the production run, thereby reducing the up front investment costs. The Hudson Jet was built on a 105 inch wheelbase, and was to be offered in three configurations: a 2-door sedan, a 4-door sedan and a convertible. In two trim levels It would be powered by 202 cu in, 104 hp, in-line six, with a 3-speed manual transmission as standard with optional overdrive and 4-speed automatic.

The new Hudson Jet compact was introduced in December 1952 at the New York City Astor Hotel. Production began in 1953. The standard 4-door sedan was priced at $1,858 and the upgraded super at $1,954 with the super 2-door sedan priced at $1,933 (there was no standard 2-door). First year sales amounted to 21,143 units. Not bad for an introductory year. But what was unforeseen and not anticipated was the industry wide slump in compact car sales. Even with the introduction of two new models, a standard 2-door sedan and a 2-door family club sedan and a new upgraded rim level the Jet Liner. Sales fell to 14, 224 units in 1954.The one bright spot was the unveiling of the Jet Liner Convertible Prototype. The convertible had a lower roof line achieved by lowering the windshield two inches. The styling boys finally got a bit of their streamlined look.

However the development together with production cost of the Jet and the cost of bringing its sporty Italia to market, put Hudson into a deep hole; with no money left to upgrade their bigger cars. Barit made a case to the board of directors that a merger was the course to take. On May 1, 1954 a merger with Nash was completed. The American Motors was born. First item of business was cutting the Jet and Italia models. Historians would muse that it was the Jet that doomed Hudson.

1953 Hudson Super Jet 4-Door

The Hudson Jet design looked a lot like a scaled down 1952-53 Ford Crestline. In the Super trim level it was available as a 4-door sedan or 2-door sedan. Fender skirts, white wall tires and wheel trim rings were optional. The 4-door pictured above, was priced at $1,954 FOB Detroit, Michigan.

1953 Hudson Standard Jet 2-Door

The 1953 standard Jet was available only as a 2-door sedan. A plain Jane model with less trim then the super model. Plain on the inside and outside. It was priced at $1,858. FOB Detroit.

The Hudson Super Jet 4-door sedan was unveiled in December 1952 at the Waldorf Astoria hotel in New York City. Production began in 1953. A total of 21,143 Jet's were built in its first year.

The compact Jet powered by a 202 cu in, 114hp in-line six made perfect sense for small town Police Departments. **Below,** the dashboard featured a instrument cluster, heater control to the left and a two spoke steering wheel with horn ring was standard. The radio and dash mounted compass were options.

1954 Hudson Italia Sports Car

The Hudson Italia Sports Coupe produced from 1954-1955 was based in the Jet platform, using many of the Jet's mechanics. Its wheelbase was 105 inches. It was designed by Hudson's design chief Frank Spring and built by Carrozzeria Touring, Milan Italy. It was priced at $4,800. Only 29 were built. After the Hudson merger with Nash in 1954. The program was discontinued.

The instrument cluster, heater controls and steering wheel were right out of the Jet. The bucket seats were ergonomic, upholstered in leather. There was no rear seat, a luggage shelf was in its place.

1954 Hudson Super Jet 4-Door

The 1954 Super Jet featured in addition to the window trim added body side molding. The fender skirts and continental spare kit were optional. Available in 2door and 4-door models.

The super Jet interior featured upgraded broadcloth upholstery and deep pile carpeting. The rear seat had room for three adults. Both the 2-door and 4-door were considered 5-passenger cars.

1954 Hudson Standard Jet 4-door

New Hudson Jet Six-Passenger, Four-Door Sedan

The basic Hudson Jet Standard 4-door Sedan. Less exterior trim. White wall tires and wheel rings and radio were optional. <u>Note:</u> roof mounted antenna. It was priced at $1,858, with 104hp six.

1954 Hudson Family Jet 2-Door Club Coupe

The plain Jane, Standard Jet Family Club Coupe. The 2-door basic model sold for $1,621, it was the lowest priced Hudson for 1954. Standard power plant was the 202 cu in, 104 hp, in-line six.

1954 Hudson Jet Utility 2-door Sedan

The stripped down Jet Utility 2-door sedan. This bare bones model was priced at $1,837 FOB Detroit. It featured bold striped cloth upholstery. <u>Note:</u> The absence of door arm rests; door handles became door pulls. Vent windows were push, pull type.

1954 Hudson Jet-Liner 4-door

The Hudson Jet Liner model was new for 1954. It featured more exterior chrome trim, standard rear fender skirts and optional continental spare. The 4-door sedan sold for $2,054 FOB Detroit.

1954 Hudson Jet-Liner 2-door

The Hudson Jet-Liner 2-door Club Sedan was one of two up-graded models that were all new for 1954. Shown here with optional 4-speed (GM) Hydramatic transmission. The base 3-speed sold for $2.046.

1954 Hudson Jet-Liner Convertible (prototype)

Only one Jet-Liner Convertible prototype was built. The model was never put into production. Based on the 2-door club coupe, with a lowered windshield, could seat six. Featured a 170 hp, twin-H , in-line six.

The Jet-Liner convertible featured an upgraded interior, with push button radio, Hydramatic transmission, color keyed steering wheel, stylized door panels and arms rests, leather upholstery, full carpeting. <u>Note:</u> the Twin-H trunk emblem and continental mounted spare tire. Priced below the Wasp it would have sold well. Too bad it was introduced in 1954 instead of 1953.

1953 Hudson Jet

Wheelbase: 105 inches   Engine: 202 cu in, 104hp in-line six*   3-speed Manual Trans.**

Model	Type	Price	Built
1C	Sedan 4-door Standard	$1,858	^

1953 Hudson Super Jet

Wheelbase: 105 inches   Engine: 202 cu in, 104hp in-line six*   3-speed Manual Trans.**

Model	Type	Price	Built
2C	Sedan 2-door Super	$1,933	^
2C	Sedan 4-door Super	1,954	^

^ Total Jet production 21,143 units. No break out by model.

1954 Hudson Jet

Wheelbase: 105 inches   Engine: 202 cu in, 104hp, in-line six*   3-speed Manual Trans.**

Model	Type	Price	Built
1D	Sedan 2-door Family Club	$1,621	^
1D	Sedan 2-door Utility	1,837	^
1D	Sedan 4-door	1,858	^

1954 Hudson Super Jet

Wheelbase: 105 inches   Engine: 202 cu in, 104hp, in-line six*   3-speed Manual Trans.**

Model	Type	Price	Built
2D	Sedan 2-door Club	$1,933	^
2D	Sedan 4-door	1,954	^

1954 Hudson Jet-Liner

Wheelbase: 105 inches   Engine: 202 cu in, 104hp, in-line six*   3-speed Manual Trans.**

Model	Type	Price	Built
3D	Sedan 2-door Club	$2,046	^
3D	Sedan 4-door	2,057	^
3D	Convertible (prototype)	N/A	Only 1 built

*Available option 106/114hp in-line six. The 170hp Twin-H standard in Convertible.
** Available option 3-speed overdrive, or Automatic (GM) Hydramatic.
^ Total Jet production 14,224 units. No break out by model.

Production, pricing and specifications from the Encyclopedia of American Cars by editors of consumer guide.

The most important new car in America!

The Henry J Sedan...See it today at your Kaiser ★ Frazer dealer's!

smart!

The Henry J's a honey on the highway...a handy helper on the farm! Note the "low waistline"... speed-style radiator grille...fluted upswept fenders. Extra-wide doors, front seat 5 feet wide! And the rear seat folds forward, giving you 55 cubic feet of space for tools, feed bags or what-have-you?

tough!

The Henry J's tough as a tractor yet nimble as a kitten! Husky Double-Channel Frame...the rear axle Hypoid-geared, as in most expensive cars! Largest vision area in any low-priced car! Short turning radius, Triple-Control Steering, oversized brakes, make it easier to handle on good roads or bad!

thrifty!

The Henry J earns its own keep! You get up to 30 to 35 miles per gallon from the quiet, responsive Supersonic Engine (choice of 4 or 6 cylinders). Lower maintenance...repair bills...insurance...operating cost! Your savings, in just two years, can more than total the down payment on the Henry J!

Built to Better the Best on the Road!

costs less to buy ... less to drive ... less to maintain!

Kaiser ★ Frazer Sales Corporation, *Willow Run, Michigan*

Kaiser Henry J
1951-1954

The idea of producing a smaller version of the Kaiser Automobile, was that of Henry J. Kaiser, Chairman and CEO of Kaiser-Frazer Corporation. Kaiser-Frazer began building and marketing an all new car at the end of World War II. Its first offering a 4-door sedan was introduced in 1946. Henry J. Kaiser was an industrialist better know for his ship building during World War II, he also established Kaiser Permanente, pioneering a preventative health system.

By 1950 production had pretty much caught up with pent-up postwar demand for new cars. To increase sales Kaiser introduced a compact version of the full size Kaiser Sedan, albeit a 2-door coupe like sedan. It was called the "Henry J", named after corporate CEO Henry J. Kaiser and designed by Howard "Dutch" Darrin.

Kaiser-Frazer Corporation obtained a loan from the Federal Government to finance production of the car. The loan came with stipulations. The car had to sell for $1,300. (Fed Tax included) it had to carry five passengers and reach 50mph. To accomplish this the "Henry J" used the fewest possible components. To save costs, there was no trunk lid, access was from behind the rear seat, the base model had no door arms rests, no glove box, one drivers side visor, fixed rear side windows and no flow through passenger ventilation. The car was introduced in September 1950, as a 1951 model and touted as "Americas first compact."

Initially the car was powered by a 134.2 cu in, 68hp, in-line 4-cyl, coupled to,a 3-speed manual transmission. Marketing for the car was aimed at the average American buyer who might only afford a used car. Advertising for the car focused on economy, The "Henry J" could achieve 25mpg. Perhaps not a prudent move, since gas was priced at 27 cents per gallon.

In 1951 a deck lid was offered as an option together with a number of up-grades. Including a 80hp in-line six, (the motor was provided by Willys and used in their CJ-3A Jeep). Two models were available in 1951, a Standard and a DeLuxe. In 1952 left over 1951 models were marketed as the Vagabond, with a continental spare added and available in two trim levels, Also available was a upgrade model called the Corsair with a standard deck lid. Kaiser convinced Sear's Roebuck to sell the Henry J badged as an Allstate through their retail stores. The Allstate had a different grille and interior. It was offered in 1952 and 1953.

By 1954 it was evident that the Henry J, was a losing proposition. The timing of its debut came at a time when buyers wanted large cars. A Chevrolet 150 could be had for less that $200 more, and gas was cheap. A total of 130,312 were built from 1950 through 1954.

1951 Henry J Standard 2-door Sedan

The basic Henry J standard sold for $1,363 in 1951 and 38,500 units were sold. <u>Note:</u> No deck lid.

Top Stars agree:
your smartest buy is *Henry J*

Ask Burns and Allen! These favorite comedians know their Henry J's reliable power, bigger vision area and oversized brakes make it one of the safest cars on the road—as well as the easiest to drive! They love the smartness that has won the Henry J the Fashion Academy Award—and marvel at its almost unbelievable thriftiness! So will *you*, when you get the facts!

Ask Ezio Pinza! Ezio Pinza's smart, spirited Henry J saves *time*—in traffic, while parking, and on the open road. And time is important to a busy star! The Henry J also saves money, with up to a fat 30 miles a gallon! In fact, what *you'd save* on initial cost, upkeep and other expenses with the Henry J could total up to $600 the first year!

Ask Risé Stevens! This lovely, world-famous singer agrees the Henry J is the world's thriftiest full-*size* car—but that's only *part* of its appeal! She loves the harmony of its sleek, smart lines and tasteful interior, its amazing durability, and the wonderfully easy way it rides and handles. For the buy of a lifetime, see the Henry J at your Kaiser-Frazer dealer's today!

$1362

Delivered at Willow Run with Federal taxes paid and local tax (if any) additional. Prices subject to change without notice.

Gem of a gift...tops in thrift

27

1951 Henry J DeLuxe 2-door Sedan

The Henry J DeLuxe featured more chrome trim around the grille and front and rear window frames. The bumper guards were standard the white walls were optional. It was priced at $1,499 and 43,400 built.

Shown above, the initial power plant was a 134.2 cu in, 68hp, in-line four..**Shown below,** is the optional 80hp, in-line six, Both engines were supplied by Willys.

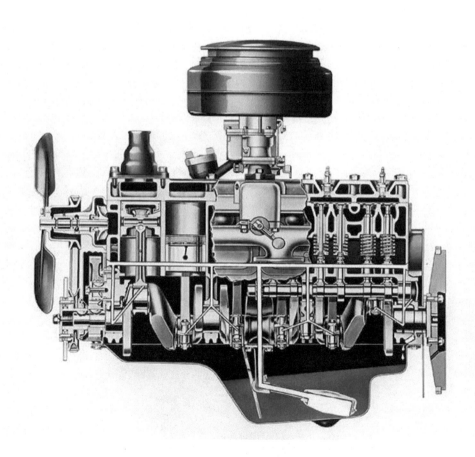

With the absence of a deck lid, trunk accessed was gained through the back seat.. **Below, the DeLuxe model featured a steering wheel with full horn ring, full carpeting, broadcloth upholstery, and column mounted gear shift.** The turn signals and radio are options. No glove box.

In 1952 Sears Roebuck began selling a re-badged Henry J . The experiment lasted two years.

Now...an American Sports car
smarter than Europe's custom models!

'52 *Henry J* Vagabond

Here at last is the car you've looked for and longed for!

It's the new Henry J Vagabond, smart new 1952 edition of America's most practical, lowest-priced, full-size car.

Outside it's a harmony of smart new colors and exciting European lines; inside, it's richly clad in new and beautiful upholsteries.

As for performance, it's definitely a car for the open road. Its Supersonic Engine eats up the miles, but scarcely touches the gasoline. (It delivers up to 30 miles per gallon.) When the lights turn green, the Vagabond's away at the head of the pack, with a new kind of flashing getaway that takes your breath away.

So...if you've always longed for a car that's young in heart, that makes you want to drive, and drive...just for the fun of it, take a demonstration ride in the new '52 Henry J Vagabond today.

Drive the new Henry J Vagabond...America's finest sports car

1952 Henry J Vagabond Standard

The 1952 Henry J Vagabond was available in two trim levels, Standard and DeLuxe. The DeLuxe had a deck lid, the standard did not. A continental spare was optional. <u>Note:</u> The continental carrier bracket with the spare laying on the ground.

1952 Henry J Vagabond Deluxe

The 1952 Henry J Vagabond DeLuxe . <u>Note:</u> the clear Lucite tube hood ornament and the deck lid with mounted continental spare. The DeLuxe sold for $1,552 and 4,000 were sold. A decrease in sales.

1952 Henry J Corsair Basic

The 1952 Henry J Corsair Basic, shown with optional white walls, full wheel covers, sun-visor and side view mirrors. The fin tail lights, deck lid, back-up lights (where tail lights used to be) and grille, all new.

1952 Henry J Corsair DeLuxe

The 1952 Henry J Corsair DeLuxe, chrome windshield and rear window moldings, bumper guards, and full wheel covers were all standard. It was priced at $1,581 approximately $162 more than the basic model. White wall tires and side view mirrors were options. The Cadillac style tail-lights and back-up lights all new.

Shown above, the Vagabond DeLuxe interior with faux alligator hide upholstery. **Below,** Corsair basic interior with bold striped cloth upholstery. Both models featured door arm rests as standard.

Your One
BRAND NEW CAR
for '52

SEARS ROEBUCK AND CO.

ALLSTATE
For All America Now!

Brand New for You in '52

SEARS ROEBUCK AND CO. **ALLSTATE** *for '53*

challenges them all *for value*

1952-1953 Allstate 2-door Sedan

Sear had previously sold an auto produced by Lincoln Motor Car back in 1908-1912. Threodore Houser Sears V.P, (who also served on K-F's board) broached the idea in 1949. After all you could buy a craftsman house through the Sears catalog. On November 20,1951 Sears announced that it would be selling the Allstate 2-door sedan, manufactured by Kaiser-Frasier. The car would be based on the compact Henry J with modifications unique to the new Allstate. Including an upscale interior, featuring: Saran plaid, leather, or smooth vinyl. Exteriors featured: full wheel covers, unique grille and hood ornament. Fitted with Allstate tires and batteries and name plates: all designed by designer Alex Tremulis. K-F dealers were encouraged to service the vehicles, none were happy at the prospect.

Three trim levels, Basic, Standard and DeLuxe and two engine options, a 68hp four and 80hp six. would be available. The Basic four sold for $1,395, which under cut the Henry J Basic Vagabond by $12. and was equipped with more standard equipment, including a operational deck lid and glove box. Sears sold the Allstate for two model years, 1952 and 1953 with total sales of only 2,363 units for the two years. The venture had failed.

The 1952 Allstate 2-door Sedan basic model.   Note: A two piece windshield, a unique grille, featuring two bars and separate parking lights, and a unique hood ornament. Wheel rings and bumper guards were standard. Also equipped with Allstate tires, batteries, spark plugs, hoses and belts. It was priced at $1,395 delivered to your local Sears Roebuck department store. The Basic was only available in 1952.

1952-1953 Allstate 2-door Standard Sedan

The 1952-1953 Allstate Standard Sedan. Shown here with optional radio, spotlight, white wall tires, fog lights and full wheel covers. The four cylinder was priced at $1.486 in 1952. In 1953 it sold for $1,528.

1952-1953 Allstate 2-door DeLuxe Sedan

The 1952-1953 Allstate DeLuxe sedan. <u>Note:</u> The unique hood ornament. The four was priced at $1,539 and the six at $1,693. In 1953 pricing was increased; the four was $1,589 and the six at $1,785.

The Allstate had a unique faux alligator vinyl and saran plaid cloth interior. Also available in all leather.

1953 Henry J Corsair 2-door Sedan

The Corsair Standard, one of two models available in1953. It was priced at $1,399 and 8,500 were built.

1953 Henry J Corsair DeLuxe 2-door Sedan

1953 Henry J DeLuxe Corsair Sedan with optional sunvisor and white wall tires. It was priced at $1,561.

Vinyl upholstery, padded dash and glove box standard. Radio and heater were options. The speedometer pod included gas and temp gauges and warning lights for amp and oil. <u>Note:</u> The manual choke on left.

1954 Henry J 2-door Sedan

Unchanged from 1953, two trim levels were available,in 1954 (its last year), Corsair Standard and Corsair DeLuxe. There was a minimal increase in price, $1,404 for the Standard and $1,556 for the DeLuxe.

1951-1952 Henry J 2-door Sedan

Wheelbase: 100 inches   Engine: 134.2 cu in, 68hp, 4-cyl*   3-speed Manual

Model	Type	Price	Built
5134	1951 Standard 2-door Sedan	$1,363	38,500
5144	1951 DeLuxe 2-door Sedan	1,499	43,400
5234	1952 Standard Vagabond 2-door	1,407	3,000
5244	1952 DeLuxe Vagabond 2-door	1,552	4,000
5234	1952 Standard Corsair 2-door	1,517	7,600
5244	1952 DeLuxe Corsair 2-door	1,664	8,900

1953-1954 Henry J 2-door Sedan

Wheelbase: 100 inches   Engine: 134.2 cu in, 68hp, 4-cyl*   3-speed Manual

Model	Type	Price	Built
5334	1953 Standard Corsair 2-door	$1,399	8,500
5344	1953 DeLuxe Corsair 2-door	1,581	8,100
5434	1954 Standard Corsair 2-door	1,404	800
5444	1954 DeLuxe Corsair 2-door	1,566	300

*Available option 161 cu in, 80hp, in-line six

1952-1953 Sears Allstate 2-door Sedan

Wheelbase: 100 inches   Engine: 134.2 cu in, 68hp, 4-cyl*   3-speed Manual

Model		Type	Price	Built
110	Series 4	1952 Basic 2-dr	$1,395	200
111	Series 4	1952 Standard 2-dr	1,486	500
113	Series 4	1952 DeLuxe 2-dr	1,539	200
114	Series 6	1952 Basic 2-dr	1,594	200
115	Series 6	1952 DeLuxe 2-dr	1,693	466
210	Series 4	1953 Standard 2-dr	1,528	200
213	Series 4	1953 DeLuxe 2-dr	1,589	225
215	Series 6	1953 DeLuxe 2-dr	1,785	372

*The series 4 referred to the four cylinder engine, the series 6 referred to the six cylinder engine.

Production, pricing and specifications from the Encyclopedia of American Cars by editors of Consumer Guide and the Standard Catalog of American Cars by John A. Gunnell.

SOMETHING ABSOLUTELY NEW

★ It's Here—a New Kind of Car offering New Beauty, Custom Luxury, Economy and Handling Ease!
★ Price Includes Weather Eye, Radio and other Custom Extras at No Extra Cost!

NOW—ALL THE THRILL OF THE OPEN CAR, WITH THE COMFORT AND SAFETY OF A SEDAN

Nash Proudly Presents the Newest Member of the Airflyte Family ...the Amazing New Rambler Convertible Landau

★ Today you can see the new Nash Rambler Custom Convertible Landau—most exciting car news in years!

Look at its continental flair—its low, racing lines. Look at its compact size—just wonderful for today's traffic. That's all new and all Nash.

★ *Look* once, and it's a weather-snug, steel-ribbed sedan. Touch a button—it's a five-passenger convertible—with the safety of overhead protection, and the quiet of rattle-proof Airflyte Construction.

And What This Car Will Do!

Just *touch* the throttle. This jewel is lightning fast with new High-Compression power. Takes you farther and faster on less gasoline than any other 5-passenger car.

And it handles like a dream, parks in a pocket, rides like a limousine!

★ The price? Here's wonderful news!

The Nash Rambler Landau comes tailored to your individual order, from a choice of custom materials— *completely equipped* with the famous Nash Weather Eye Conditioned Air System, built-in radio and other custom extras as standard equipment. *Yet costs less than any other five-passenger convertible on the market today.*

★ Come *see* this new member of the Nash Airflyte family. Ask your Nash dealer for the keys to the newest thrill on wheels.

THERE'S MUCH OF TOMORROW IN ALL NASH DOES TODAY

THE AMBASSADOR
Available with Hydra-Matic Drive

THE STATESMAN
White sidewall tires optional extra

All 3 Nash Airflytes, including the Rambler, feature Airflyte Construction—entire frame and body are a single, welded unit, rattle-proof, double-rigid. Stays new years longer.

Nash Airflyte

The Ambassador ☆ The Statesman ☆ The Rambler
Nash Motors. Division Nash-Kelvinator Corp. Detroit, Mich.

1950-1954 Nash Rambler

George W. Mason, President of Nash was looking for a way to compete with the Big Three U.S. Auto Makers in the post World War II market. What he wanted was something more cost effective, without giving up any amenities. What he settled on was a design by Nashes Meade Moore of engineering and Theodore Ulrich of styling. A unibody design that was smaller and lighter, but could still carry 5 passengers in comfort. Nash could save money on production and customers could save on fuel. The proposed car was in keeping with Nash's full size FireFlyte designed cars, but smaller. A convertible with a wheelbase of 100 inches, powered by the proven 173 cu in, 82hp, L-head six. The light weight car could deliver 30mpg. It was given the name Rambler, a name from its past 1897 prototype. It was heralded as the Rambler Custom Landau Convertible Coupe and introduced on April 13, 1950, in the middle of the model year. It was priced at $1,808. A Station Wagon, was added on June 23,1950. A total of 11,042 units were sold in its first short year.

In 1951 the Rambler line up was enlarged and included: the Convertible, the Station Wagon and a pillar-less Hardtop Coupe. Two trim levels were available, the Custom and the Super. The entry level Rambler was the Super Station Wagon priced at $1,885. The only model available in this trim level. Upgraded models were the, Custom Convertible at $1,993, the Custom Station Wagon at $1,993 and the Custom Country Club Hardtop Coupe at $1,968. A total of 68,762 units were sold. Mason got it right.

With no real changes since 1950. In 1952 Rambler introduced the Deliveryman, a utility wagon fitted with sold steel panels instead of glass quarter windows. In the Custom series a special Edition Greenbriar Station Wagon was made available, in honor of famed golfer Sam Snead. It had a special two tone green paint scheme and was priced at $2,119. The popularity of the Rambler was solidified by a total of 53,000 units sold.

For 1953 the Rambler received a facelift: It looked more like the full size Nash line-up. The new Airflyte styling was from the designer Battista 'Pinin' Farina. With a flying lady hood ornament designed by none other than George Petti (famed WW II pin-up artist). Engine power was increased to 85hp with an optional 90hp six available. GM Hydra-Matic transmission was optional, Nash's Weather Eye heating / ventilating system was standard in Custom models. Convertibles and hardtops received a continental spare at no additional cost. Advertising was steered toward the Rambler as a second car, aimed at the growing sub-urban family.

In 1954 the Rambler model line-up was expanded to include: 2-door and 4-door sedans, and 2-door and 4-door station wagons. A total of ten trim levels were available. A total of 36,175 units were sold. The Big Three, GM, Ford and Chrysler, announced drastic price cuts. Competition was fierce. On May 1, 1954 Nash and Hudson had entered into a merger agreement. The new company would be called American Motors.

1950 Rambler Landau Convertible

The 1950 Rambler Landau Convertible. Shown here with white wall tires, AM radio, full wheel covers, and electric clock were standard. <u>Note:</u> the top in the Landau position. It could be fully retracted and stored behind the rear seat back. A total of 9,330 were sold in the six month abbreviated first model year.

In the full up position the top was completely weather tight as a sedan. The frame above the windows served as the top rails and housed the operating cables, and kept the body ridged without adding extra bracing. The top was electrically operated. Classified as a 5-passenger, but 4 would fit comfortably.

The convertible interior featured: premium two tone cloth upholstery, two sun visors, deluxe steering wheel with horn ring, door arm rests and a under dash drawer in place of a glove box. The gear shifter was column mounted. Full carpeting front and rear. The electric clock and radio were options.

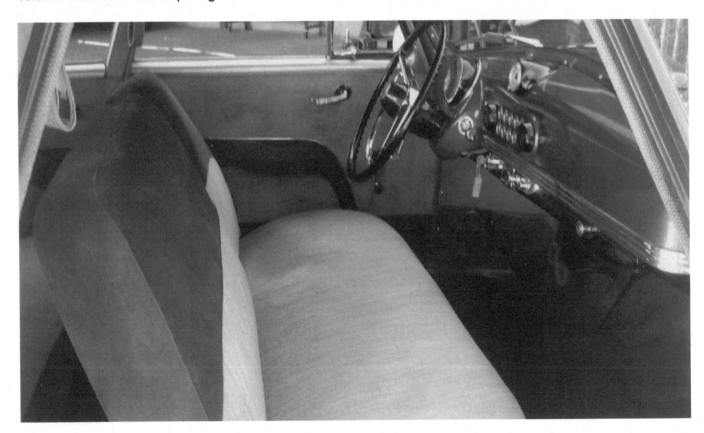

1950 Rambler Custom Station Wagon

The Rambler Custom Station Wagon was introduced on June 23, 1950, three months after the convertible. An all steel 2-door model that featured 3M simulated wood trim. <u>Note:</u> Optional accessory roof rack.

Controls under the radio operate the Nash Weather Eye heat and ventilation system. Interior was upholstered in pin stripe broadcloth. Rear seat back folds down for added cargo space.

1951-1952 Rambler Custom Convertible

1951-1952 Rambler Custom Convertible was unchanged. In 1951 it was priced at $1,993 in 1952 it was $2,119. A total of 18,367 were sold. Note: The rear deck name plate. All Nash's were referred to as Airflyte, which denoted its styling. Maintaining the side rails helped with the overall integrity.

1951-1952 Rambler Custom Country Club Hardtop

The Rambler Custom Country Club 2-door Hardtop was introduced as part of the Custom series in 1951. Features included a wraparound three piece rear window. The smart looking car was a big hit and a total of 45,101 were sold over the two year period. Out selling the convertible by nearly 27,000 units.

1951-1952 Rambler Custom Station Wagon

The 1951-1952 Rambler Custom Station Wagon with 3M wood grain applique. 48,507 were sold.

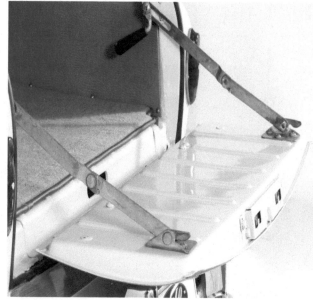

The wood grain trim was a 3m applique. Cargo area egress was via a left gate / tailgate combination. The hood scoop was part of the Weather Eye system. A spring loaded hood hinge negated a hood rod support. The heavy chrome Nash crest was part of the grille assembly, 1952 last year used.

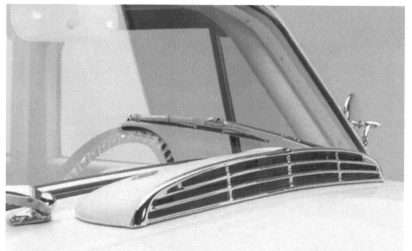

The Custom Station Wagon interior was unchanged. Electric clock and AM radio and smooth two tone upholstery and full carpeting. The steering wheel with horn ring and door arm rests, standard.

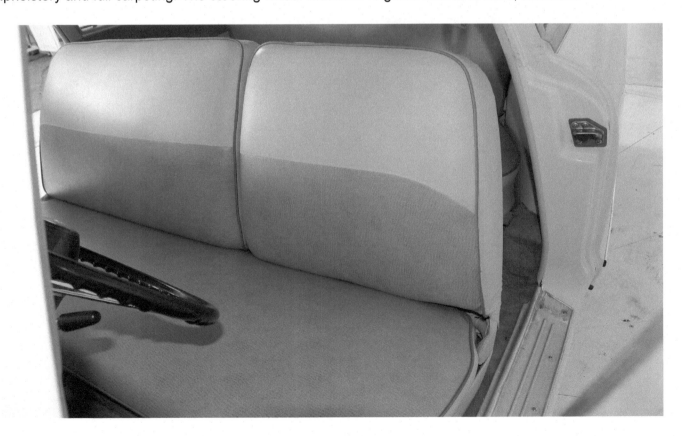

Shown here is the standard engine for all years, all models the 172.6 cu in, 82hp, L-Head in-line six cyl.

1952 Rambler Greenbrier Station Wagon

The 1952 Special Edition Greenbrier Station Wagon painted a two tone green paint scheme. The wagon was named after the famed hotel resort. It was part of the custom series sold in limited numbers.

Golf great Sam Sean is pictured with the Greenbrier Station Wagon. Note: The Greenbrier script on lower front fender. **Below,** the two tone color scheme was carried into the interior, dash, door panels and seats.

1951-1954 Rambler Super Suburban Wagon

The Super Suburban Wagon was more of a utility wagon, much like the SUV of today. Introduced in 1951 it was available through 1954. The lowest priced Rambler. <u>Note:</u> Accessory roof rack.

1953-1954 Custom Convertible Coupe

In 1953 the Rambler received a major face-lift. New grille, new bumpers, tail lights, hood scoop and a continental spare was added to the convertible and hardtop. By 1953 convertible sales had dropped dramatically. With 3,284 sold in 1953 and only 221 in 1954, it's last year. Prices were slashed to no avail.

1953-1954 Rambler Custom Station Wagon

The Rambler station wagon was once again a leading seller for 1953-1954. Over 23,400 units were sold for the two years. In 1953-1954 two trim levels were available; the Super and Custom. The 1953 Super was priced at $2,003, the Custom $2,119. In 1954 prices were reduced to$1,800 for the Super and $1,950 for the Custom. The Petty designed hood ornament and white wall tires were optional.

1953-1954 Rambler Custom Country Club Hardtop

The Custom Country Club hardtop coupe was the best seller for 1953 having sold more than 16,800 units.
<u>Note:</u> The rear bumper of the Rambler looks like it belongs on the front and vise versa.

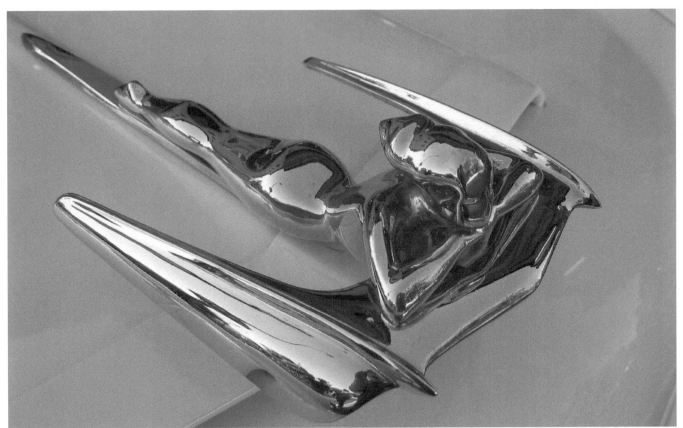

In 1953 Rambler received what it called "Airflyte" re-styling. The compacts now looked more like the full size models. The new style was done by Italian designer Pinin Farina. Nash also commissioned famed pinup artist George Petty to design a new 'Flying Lady' hood ornament. The new styling included a new dashboard. A recessed feature panel housed the radio and electric clock. <u>Note:</u> Emergency brake handle.

1954 Ramber Custom 4-door Sedan

Introduced in 1954 the Rambler 4-door sedan was available in either the Super and Custom trim level. The Super sold for $1,795 and the Custom for $1,965. A total of 11,953 were produced.

1954 Rambler Cross Country Wagon

New for 1954 was the Rambler Cross Country 4-door Station Wagon, it was the most expensive and most popular model in a expanded line-up. Priced at $2,050 a total of 9,039 were sold in its first year.

The dip in the rear roof panel was filled with a roof rack, which became standard on future Rambler wagons. The dip was signature design created by Bill Reddig. With the addition of the roof rack cargo capacity had increased considerably. The wagon carried 5 passengers comfortably.

70

1954 Rambler 2-door Sedan

New for 1954 was the Rambler 2-door Sedan. Available in the DeLuxe or upgraded Super trim levels. The DeLuxe was the entry level model priced at $1,550 and the Super sold for $1,700

1950-1951-1952 Rambler

Wheelbase: 100 inches Engine: 172.6 cu in, 82hp, L-head in-line six   3-speed Manual

Model	Year	Type	Price	Built
5021	1950	Custom Landau Convertible	$1,808	9,330
5024	1950	Custom Station Wagon	1,806	1,712
5114	1951	Super Suburban Wagon	1,885	5,568
5121	1951	Custom Convertible	$1,993	15,259
5124	1951	Custom Wagon 2-dr	1,993	28,618
5127	1951	Custom Cntry Club Htp Cpe	1,988	19,317
5214	1952	Super Suburban Wagon	$2,003	2,970
5221	1952	Custom Convertible	2,119	3,108
5224	1952	Custom Wagon 2-dr	2,119	19,889
5227	1952	Custom Cntry Club Htp Cpe	2,094	25,784

1953-1954 Rambler

Wheelbase: 100 inches Engine: 184.0 cu in, 85hp, L-head in-line six*   3-speed Manual**

Model	Year	Type	Price	Built
5314	1953	Super Suburban Wagon	$2,003	1,114
5321	1953	Custom Convertible	2,150	3,284
5324	1953	Custom Wagon 2-dr	2,119	10,571
5327	1953	Custom Cntry Club Htp Cpe	2,125	16,809
5406	1954	DeLuxe 2-dr Sedan	$1,550	7,273
5414	1954	Super Suburban Wagon	1,800	504
5415	1954	Super 4-dr Sedan	1,795	4,313
5416	1954	Super 2-dr Sedan	1,700	300
5417	1954	Super Cntry Club Htp Cpe	1,800	1,071
5421	1954	Custom Convertible	1,980	221
5424	1954	Custom Wagon 2-dr	1,950	2,202
5425	1954	Custom 4-dr Sedan	1,965	7.640
5427	1954	Custom Cntry Club Htp Cpe	1,950	3,612
5428	1954	Custom Cross Cntry Wgn 4-dr	2,050	9,039

*Standard in 4-dr and cars equipped with Hydra-Matic.
** Optional Hydra-Matic transmission.

Pricing, production and specifications information from Encyclopedia of American Cars by Editors of Consumer Guide and Standard Catalog of American Cars by John A. Gunnell.

WHAT DOES THIS GRILLE SIGNIFY?

➤ This grille performs a vital function by admitting an unrestricted flow of air to the radiator. It's an attractive grille by virtue of its entirely functional shape and it signifies what other grilles do not . . . that this is an honest car dealing in fundamentals.

➤ The Lark has an unusually high brake lining to weight ratio, and employs an advanced suspension system using variable rate coil springs and hydraulic shocks. Only 14½ feet long, it seats six comfortably and is extremely maneuverable, very easy to park and agile in traffic.

➤ Like to work on your own car? The Lark's engine ("6" or V-8) is easily accessible. ➤ Like economy? The Lark V-8 outclassed all V-8's in the Mobilgas Economy Run: 22.28 miles per gallon with automatic transmission. And the "6" does better. ➤ Like performance? Try The Lark V-8 with 4-barrel carburetor and dual exhausts. ➤ Like to drive? Get into a Lark. ➤ See your Studebaker Dealer.

THE LARK BY STUDEBAKER

1959-1963 Studebaker Lark

The merger of Studebaker and Packard had proved to be a mistake, the company had been losing money since inception. Subsequently the company entered into a management contract with Curtiss-Wright Aircraft Company with a promise of a takeover. It was not the rescue they had hoped for, in fact things got worse, with Curtiss-Wright siphoning off prime assets. It was at this time that Studebaker President Harold E. Churchill convinced the Board of Directors that what Studebaker needed to rescue their automobile business, was a compact car, sighting the success of AMC with the Rambler. The problem; a lack of funds for such a project. The Company was bleeding cash daily. There was not enough money for a much needed major change to existing models, a new model was out of reach. But Churchill had an unique idea; taking an existing full size body shell and keeping the cabin compartment, shorting the wheelbase, applying new sheet metal to the quarter panels, deck lid and front clip. A compact model for six passengers could be achieved at minimal cost. The Board approved Churchill's concept and the Studebaker Lark was born.

The Lark was introduced in the fall of 1958 as a 1959 model. It was available as a 2-door sedan, 4-door sedan, 2-door hardtop coupe and 2-door wagon, in two trim levels: Deluxe and Regal. The Lark was powered by two standard engines: 90hp six and 180hp V-8 plus an optional 195hp V-8.

For 1959 Studebaker had gambled by dropping all full size models except the 2-door Silver Hawk and went all in with the Lark. The gutsy move paid off; 131,078 Lark's and 7,788 Hawk's were sold. Excluding American Motors, Studebaker had more compact models than any other U.S. auto maker.

In 1960 a convertible and 4-door station wagon were introduced. The 4-door wagon was available in entry level Deluxe trim and upgraded Regal trim. The convertible was available in Regal trim only. The Hawk coupe was available only with a 210hp V-8. The Silver part was dropped. Industry wide Ford had introduced its compact, the Falcon and Chevrolet introduced the compact Corvair. Chrysler debuted their compact in 1960 as the Valiant. Studebaker sales dipped slightly to 130,365 units.

For 1961 Studebaker added a upscale 4-door Cruiser sedan. It was priced at $2,458 and available with 180hp V-8 as standard with a 195hp V-8 optional. Sales fell to 70,309 units. In 1962 a third trim level was added, the upscale Daytona, two models were available; a hardtop coupe and convertible coupe. Convertibles and hardtops were now available in two upscale trim levels; Regal and Daytona. Sales increased to 101,392 units.

In 1963 trim levels were reshuffled. The Deluxe became the Standard, and a new upgraded level between the Regal and Daytona; the Custom was added. Two models were available in the Custom trim, a 2-door sedan and 4-door sedan. New for 1963 was the Grand Turismo Hawk and the Avanti. Lark sales fell to 73,192 units. In 1964 the Lark name plate was dropped and by 1966 the Studebaker automobile was gone.

1959-61 Lark 2-door Sedan

For 1959-1961 the 2-door sedan was available in Deluxe trim only. It was smart looking and could accommodate 6 passengers comfortably. It was the least expensive Lark and the only 2-door 6 passenger compact available in 1959. In 1960 Ford introduced the Falcon 2-door 6 passenger sedan. It would be the Lark's nose to nose competitor, and priced $64 less than the Lark.

A unique feature of the 2-door Lark sedan; roll down quarter windows and a one piece, wrap around, rear window. A feature usually found in larger, full size cars. For its size, 6-passengers rode comfortably.

The 2-door sedan featured a stylish interior with velour upholstered seating. <u>Note:</u> The placement of the glove box. The center tunnel was wide, allowing for comfortable front seating for three.

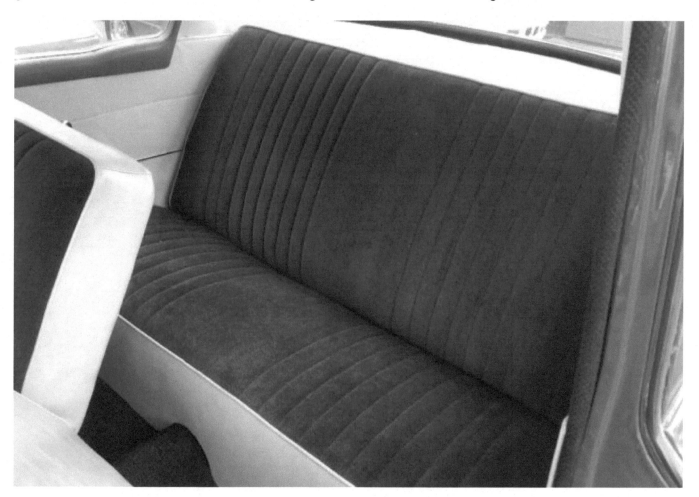

1959-1961 Lark 4-door Sedan

The Lark 4-door sedan was available in two trim levels; the Deluxe and Regal. Shown here is the Regal, with optional white wall tires and full wheel covers. The interior had an upgrade in upholstery trim.

1961 Lark Cruiser 4-door Sedan

Introduced in 1961, the Lark Cruiser 4-door sedan, with a longer wheelbase, would be the luxury sedan for the next two years. <u>Note:</u> The quad headlights, (Regal and Cruiser models all received quad headlights) rear door operational vent windows and special upscale upholstery. The Cruiser was priced at $2,458

1959-1961 Lark Hardtop Coupe

The Lark 2-door hardtop shared the same roof line as the sedan without the 'B' pillar. Introduced in 1959 it was available in Regal trim only, with six cylinder or V-8 configuration through 1961. In1959 the smart looking six cylinder version was priced at $2,275, in 1960 it sold for $2,296 and in 1961 it sold for $2,243.

In 1961 a padded dash was added. The interior was upholstered in pleated vinyl. A 3-speed manual was standard, overdrive and "Flightomatic" automatic transmissions were options.

1961-1964 Lark Skytop

First introduced in 1961 the folding SkyTop option was available through 1964 on sedan and hardtop models, at $185. <u>Note:</u> How the roof panel was flattened on both models. Shown **below** is the 1962-64 model. Front bucket seats and a center console was introduced on 2-door hardtops in 1962.

1959-61 Lark 2-door Wagon

The Lark 2-door Station Wagon was available in six cyl or V-8 version, in standard Deluxe or Regal Trim.

1960-1961 Lark 4-door Wagon

The Lark 4-door Station Wagon in Deluxe or Regal trim, with either six cyl or V-8 were introduced in 1960. Station wagons rode on a longer 113 inch wheelbase. The 1961 tailgate window was framed in chrome.

Upper left, 169.6 cu in, 90hp flat head six available 1959-1960. **Upper right,** 169.6 cu in, 112 hp, OHV six available from 1961-1963. **Below,** the 289.2 cu in, 180hp was the standard V-8 from 1959-1963.

85

1962-1963 Lark 2-door Sedan

In 1962 the wheelbase was increased to 113 inches. Two series were identified by engine, The Lark Six or the Lark Eight. The 2-door sedan was offered in both. The Six 2-door was priced at $1,935 and the Eight at $3,070. Both sported a new, Mercedes like, grille with hood ornament and new rear with round taillights.

1962-1963 Lark 4-door Sedan

The 4-door sedan was available in both the Six and Eight series. In 1962 the trim offered for both were DeLuxe and Regal. In 1963 the trim packages were changed to Standard and Regal. The 1962 Eight Regal was priced at $2,325 and in 1963 is was priced at $2,685.

1962-1963 Lark Cruiser 4-door Sedan

The 4-door Cruiser sedan was offered only in the Lark Eight series. This was the top-of-the line sedan. In 1962 it was priced at $2,493 and in 1963 at $2,595. Hood ornament and grille were a Mercedes influence.

1962-1963 Lark 2-door Hardtop

The Lark hardtop coupe was available in the Six and Eight series. The 1963 Daytona Six shown here, was priced at $2,308. The hardtop coupe was also available with Regal trim in 1962. In 1963 available only with Daytona trim in both the Six and Eight series. White wall tires were optional.

1962-1963 Lark Convertible

The Lark convertible was available in the Six and Eight series with both Regall and Daytona trim, in 1962. In 1963 it was only offered in Daytona trim in both series. Radio and side view mirrors were optional.

The Lark convertible shown here in Daytona trim, sporting luxury two-tone pleated vinyl seats. Bucket seats, center console, wall-to-wall carpeting and seat belts were all standard. Side mirrors, optional.

New for 1962-1963 round tail lights, with oblong backup lights, wire wheel covers, a smart looking hood ornament, and rear gravel shield. The full size spare took up a lot of cargo space.

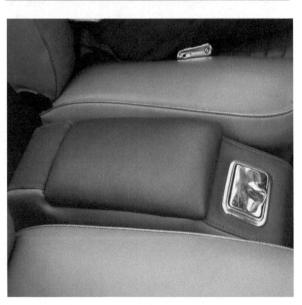

The dashboard shown **above** was new for 1962. <u>Note:</u> The optional A/C unit and the floor mounted stick shift. **Below,** in 1963 the dash was once again changed.

93

1962-1963 Lark Station Wagon

In 1962 the Wagon was available in the Six and Eight series in both DeLuxe and Regal trim. In 1963 the wagon was available in both Six and Eight series with Standard, Deluxe and Daytona trim. <u>Note:T</u>the pronounced tail lights and back-up lights. The side trim seems to fade into the panel bump outs, awkward.

In 1963 an additional wagon model was available, mid-year, with a unique sliding rear roof panel, called the Wagonair. It was priced $100. higher than the Daytona model. <u>Note:</u> The 1964 tail lights.

1960 Lark Italian Style

In 1960 Italian Studebaker importer Renato Bornigia commissioned Italian designer Pietro Frura of Torino to design an alternative to the then current Duncan MacRae production design. Two prototypes were built, a 2-door coupe and a 4-door sedan. Both cars were to be powered by V-8s. None went into production.

1962 Studebaker Scepter Concept

The 1962 Sceptre Concept was designed by Brooks Stevens. It featured a full length non glare headlight, by Sylvania. The design was sanction for possible production in 1966. Sadly it was not to be.

The interior of the Spectre featured a space age dashboard, leather bucket seats, a glove box drawer that turned into a vanity, floor shifter and center armrest. <u>Note:</u> The speedometer long bar that sat on the dash.

1959-1960-1961 Studebaker Lark

Wheelbase: 108.5 / 113 in.		Engine: 169.6 cu in, 90hp, in-line six*	3-speed manual**	
Model	type	Price / Year^		Built
59S/V	Deluxe Sedan 4-door	$1,995 1959 / $2.046 1960 / $1,935 1961		^^
	Deluxe Sedan 2-door	$1,925 1959 / $1,976 1960 / $2,005 1961		^^
	Deluxe Wagon 2-dr	$2,295 1959 / $2,366 1960 / $2,290 1961		^^
	Deluxe Wagon 4-dr	$2,441 1960 / $2,576 1961		^^
	Regal Sedan 4-door	$2,175 1959 / $2,196 1960 / $2,155 1961		^^
	Regal HT Coupe	$2,411 1959 / $2,296 1960 / $2,243 1961		^^
	Regal Wagon 2-door	$2,455 1959 / $2,590 1960 / $2,370 1961		^^
	Regal Wagon 4-door	$2,591 1960 / $2,520 1961		^^
	Cruiser Sedan 4-door	$2,458 1961		^^

^six cylinder pricing shown, V-8 pricing aprox 7% higher
*optional 180hp V-8 and 195hp V-8
** Automatic Transmission optional
^^Total production 1959 138,866 and 1960 1131,654 and 1961 70,309 includes 2-door Hawk.

1962-1963 Studebaker Lark

Wheelbase: 113 inches		Engine:169.6 cu in, 112hp, in-line Six*	3-speed manual**	
Model	Type	Price/ Year^		Built
62/3S/v	DeLuxe sedan 4-door	$2.040 1962		^^
	Standard sedan 4-dr	$2,040 1963		^^
	DeLuxe sedan 2-door	$1,935 1962		^^
	Standard Sedan 2-dr	$1,935 1963		^^
	DeLuxe Wgn 4-Door	$2,405 1962		^^
	Standard Wgn 4-dr	$2,430 1963		^^
	Regal sedan 4-door	$2,190 1962/ $2,160 1963		^^
	Regal Wgn 4-door	$2,555 1962/ $2,550 1963		^^
	Regal HT coupe	$2,218 1962		^^
	Regal sedan 2-dr	$2,055 1963		^^
	Custom sedan 4-dr	$2,285 1963		^^
	Custom sedan 2-dr	$2,180 1963		^^
	Daytona HT coupe	$2,308 1962/ $2,308 1963		^^
	Daytona Cvt coupe	$2,679 1962/ $2,679 1963		^^
	Dyatona Wgn 4-dr	$2,700 1963		^^
62/3V	Crusier 4-door	$2,493 1962/ $2,595 1963		^^

^ Six cylinder pricing shown, V-8 pricing aprox 7% higher.
* Optional 180 V-8, 195 V-8, 210 V-8 and 225 V-8
** Automatic Transmission optional
^^ Total production Six and Eight 1962 91,004 , 1963 73,192

Pricing and production information from Standard Catalog of American Cars by John a. Gunnell.

Almost Like Flying!

The New Aero Willys

LOAFS AT 60 – CRUISES AT 75 – WITH POWER TO SPARE

UP TO 35 MILES PER GALLON WITH OVERDRIVE

DRIVER SEES ALL FOUR FENDERS

First Car to Combine Such Luxury With Record Mileage!
A blend of aero and auto engineering has created in the
Aero Willys a new *kind* of car! Its ride is so cloud-soft and
luxurious, you feel airborne. When you press the accelerator,
it almost seems to sprout wings. Yet this amazing car gives
mileage up to 35 miles per gallon in overdrive*! Before you
buy any car in any class, drive an *Aero* Willys.
WILLYS-OVERLAND MOTORS, Toledo, Ohio.

*TAKE AN "AIRBORNE" RIDE
AT ANY WILLYS DEALER'S*

Equipment, specifications and trim subject to change without notice. *Optional
equipment, and white sidewall tires,
extra. Factory axle ratio available.

61-Inch-Wide Seating, both front
and rear, provides luxurious spacious-
ness for six full-grown passengers.

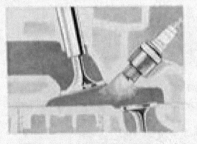

F-Head Hurricane 6 Engine with 7.6
compression tops all other American
sixes in efficiency of power output.

Willys builds for defense
—military Jeeps, aircraft
parts, many other products.

1952-1954 Willys Aero

Better known for the Jeep, Willys-Overland Company had produced passenger cars from 1937 to 1942. Military Jeeps from 1942, Civilian Jeeps from 1946. Willys re-entered the passenger car market in 1952, introducing a new uni-body compact car, the Aero.

Initially the 1952 Willys offered a 2-door sedan, the Aero, with a wheelbase of 108 inch. It was powered by either a 6 cylinder L-head, 161 cu in, 75hp engine or a 6 cylinder F-head 161 cu in, 90hp engine. Later in the year the sedan was joined by a 2-door Hardtop coupe. The entry level Aero was called the Lark. It was priced at $1,731 and 7,474 were sold. The Median level was called the Wing, it sold for $1,989 and 12,819 were sold. The up-grade level 2-door sedan was called the Ace, it sold for 2,074 and 8,706 were sold. The 2-door Hardtop was called the Eagle and it had a price tag of 2,155, only 2,364 were sold. Total 1952 model year production amounted to 31,363, a slow start for a seasoned manufacturer.

In 1953 Willys introduced the Aero 4-door sedan, the trim levels, from entry to top level, in that order were called: Lark, Ace, Eagle and Falcon. A 2-door and 4-door sedan were available in the Lark, Ace and Falcon levels, while the 2-door hardtop was only available in the Eagle trim level. A new 134.2 cu in, 72hp 4 cylinder was introduced. The 72hp 4cyl and the 75 hp 6cyl were standard in the Lark. The 75hp 6cyl was standard in the Falcon level, and the 90hp 6cyl was standard in the Ace and Eagle levels. Total production for 1953 amounted to 35,378, a slight increase, but still anemic. On April 28, 1953 Willys became a subsidiary of Kaiser Industries.

There was a realignment of series models and trim levels in 1954. The Lark series had two models and two trim levels. There were 2-door and 4-door sedans with either Standard or Deluxe trim. The Ace series had 2-door and 4-door sedan with Standard, DeLuxe or Custom trim. The Eagle series had one model, the hardtop coupe. With four trim levels; the Standard, DeLuxe, Custom and Special. Total production for 1954 was a dismal 11,709 units.

In 1955 its final year the Aero name was dropped, all passenger cars were simply referred to as Willys. The series were pared down to three; the Ace, Custom and Bermuda, with only one trim level for all; Standard. The entry level Ace, had one model a 4-door sedan. The mid-series had two models; a 2-door sedan and a 4-door sedan, The Bermuda had one model the hardtop coupe. With only 5,106 cars sold, Kaiser Willys closed down its passenger car line and moved tooling to Brazil.

In 1963 Kaiser changed the company name to Kaiser-Jeep Corporation, (the Willys name was gone thereafter). In 1970 Kaiser Jeep sold out to American Motors. In 1987 Chrysler purchase AMC and later Chrysler Fiat, following Daimler Chrysler, acquired the Jeep name.

1952-1954 Willys Aero 2-door sedan

The Willys-Aero 2-door sedan was available from 1952 -1955. In 1952 it was available in three trim levels. In 1953 in four trim levels, in 1954 in three level and in 1955 only one trim level; Standard. The driving lights and side mirror, antenna and white wall tires were optional. Price ranged from $1,731 in 1952 to $1,725 in 1955.

1952-1954 Willys Aero 2-door Hardtop

Shown here is the 1953 model 2-door hardtop coupe. A one piece curved windshield was featured, replacing the 2 piece glass of the previous year. Wheel cover centers were painted red and the "W" emblem was gold.

"This my wife would never understand"

"Well, it was like this. I was the sort who knew his own mind, knew what he wanted. Didn't ask advice often, particularly at home. Seeing that beauty on the street was what woke me up to what I'd been missing. Here I'd been buying the same old kind of car, year after year, never asking the little woman what she wanted. Man, that Aero Willys made me realize that something's happened in the automobile business. When I saw that car, and realized how beautiful it was . . . how it was made by Willys Motors who made the 'Jeep' famous . . . I determined to buy an Aero Willys for my wife. It wasn't even her birthday, (and I don't think it was an anniversary of any kind) that's why she can't understand it. But is she happy with her new **AERO WILLYS**"

TO UNDERSTANDING HUSBANDS:
Escort your wife to a Willys show-
room today. We'll do the rest!

© 1953, Willys Motors, Inc., Toledo

1953-1954 Willys Aero 4-door Sedan

The 1953 Willys-Aero Falcon, The 4-door sedan was introduced this year. The full wheel covers were standard in this trim level. Price of the 4-door sedan ranged from$1,732 in 1953 to 1,795 in 1955.

The dashboard featured a speedometer pod with gauges. Heater controls were under dash, a cigar lighter was placed next to the ashtray and the glove box was a drawer. <u>Note:</u> The wiper knob with washer button.

HURRICANE 6 (left) "The engine is almost unbeatable for efficiency, producing .560 brake-horsepower for each cubic inch of its size"—says a leading motor magazine. Such highly efficient use of gas comes from the better "breathing" of its F-head design (large overhead intake valve and valve-in-block exhaust) ... its cast-in-block, heat-regulated intake manifold ... and its high, 7.6-to-1 compression, which does not require premium gas. In the *Aero-Eagle* and *Aero-Ace*, this 90-horsepower engine gives flashing acceleration at all speeds and mileage unmatched by any 6-cylinder American car—you can drive 400 to 500 miles on a tankful. It is one of the truly great engines of the entire world.

LIGHTNING 6 (right) The 75-horsepower *Lightning 6 Engine*, power plant of the *Aero-Falcon* and *Aero-Lark*, has been proved in millions of miles of service in the famous Willys Station Wagon. Now in the *Aero* Willys, the *Lightning 6* provides dependable service, long life and excellent fuel and oil economy.

Extra-long front coil springs, rubber cushioned, smooths road roughness to give you a smooth, "airborne" ride that rivals the comfort of the largest cars.

The 161 cu in, 90hp F-head 6cyl shown **above** and the 134.2 cu in, 72hp, in-line 4cyl shown **below.**

1954 Willys Aero Custom 2-door

In 1954 the Aero Lark received a minor face lift, it featured; a curved windshield, wrap around back glass new tail lights, hidden deck lid hinges, new headlight bezels and a new dashboard and interior.

Shown **above** the 4-door sedan introduced in 1953 had a one piece back glass. **Below** the 2-door had a three piece wrap around back glass. <u>Note:</u> The exposed deck lid hinges. They were hidden in 1954.

In 1954 some 2-door models, including the hardtop had a one piece warp around back glass. In 1955 all models had the one piece wrap around back glass. The 4-door sedan shown **below**. <u>Note:</u> Deck lid hinges were no longer exposed. The overall design received a major face lift, and a reduction in models.

Now You Can Own this Smart 'Hardtop' at Less than the Price of an Ordinary Sedan

WILLYS

LOWEST PRICED "HARDTOP"
FOR 1955

$1795

ADVERTISED DELIVERY PRICE

Includes Federal Tax and Delivery Charges. State and Local Taxes (if any). Optional Equipment and Freight, Extra. Tubeless Tires, Standard Equipment—White Sidewalls Extra.

*

TAKE A SHARP LOOK AT THE
1955 WILLYS 4-DOOR SEDAN

The Willys Custom 4-Door, at its newly-lowered price for 1955 is one car you must see this year. Compare its roominess, performance and value with anything near its price, today! WILLYS MOTORS, INC., Toledo 1, Ohio.

THESE ARE THE VALUE YARDSTICKS THAT MAKE WILLYS A GREAT BUY

ECONOMY Low first cost; high gas mileage from big power-to-weight ratio; low repair and maintenance record, make this the thrift buy.

VISIBILITY Three years ago, Willys pioneered 4-fender visibility for the driver. Aero design lets you see road 10 feet ahead of bumper.

SAFETY Low gravity center, aero-frame construction, huge glass area, combine to make Willys one of the safest cars on the road.

BEAUTY More than skin deep, its sleek *individual* beauty is matched only by its beautiful performance on highway and boulevard.

$1725

ADVERTISED DELIVERY PRICE

Includes Federal Tax and Delivery Charges. State and Local Taxes (if any). Optional Equipment and Freight, Extra. Tubeless Tires, Standard Equipment.

SEE THESE TWO GREAT VALUE LEADERS AT WILLYS DEALERS NOW

55

1955 Willys Custom 4-door

The 1995 Willys received a major face lift. Shown here is the Custom 4-door sedan priced at $1,795.

1955 Willys Custom 2-door

Shown here is an early Eagle Custom with an extra belt line molding over the rear quarter. The continental spare was standard on the 1954 Eagle DeLuxe Custom. In 1955 it was an option.

1955 Willys Bermuda Hardtop Coupe

The 1955 Willys Bermuda hardtop coupe was the flagship model. It sold for $1,997 and 2,156 were built.
Willys ceased building U.S. Passenger cars in April 1954 and all production shifted to Willys de Barsil.

The new dash was introduced in 1954. The sedan was upholstered in soft pin-striped Mohair. The Bermuda hardtop was upholstered in tow tone vinyl. The trunk was adequate and covered with a vinyl mat. USA production of the Willys Aero ended in April 1954, but continued in Brazil through 1962.

1952-1953 Willys Aero

Wheelbase: 108 inches	Engine: 161 cu in 75hp in-line 6 cylinder*		3-speed Manual**
Model	Type	Price 1952/1953	Built 1952/ 1953`
652	Lark 2-door sedan	$1,731/ 1,646	7,474/ 8,205
	Wing 2-door sedan	$1,989/	12,819/
	Ace 2-door sedan	$2,074/ 1,963	8,706/ 4,988
	Ace 4-door sedan	/ 2,038	/ 7,475
	Eagle Hardtop Coupe	$2,155/ 2,157	2,364/ 7,018
	Falcon 2-door sedan	/ 1,760	/ 3,064
	Falcon 4-door sedan	/ 1,861	/ 3,117

*Option 161 cu in, 90hp 6cyl and standard on 1953 Lark 134.2 cu in, 72hp, 4cyl.
**Overdrive optional.

1954-1955 Willys Aero

Wheelbase: 108 inches	Engine: 134.2 cu in, 72hp, 4 cylinder*		3-speed Manual**
Model	Type	Price 1954/ 1955	Built 1954/ 1955
654	Lark 2-dr sedan	$1,737/	1,482/
	Lark 4-dr sedan	$1,823/	1,370/
	Ace 2-dr sedan	$1,892/1,856	1,380/ 6
	Ace 4-dr sedan	$1,968/	1,195/
	Ace Dlx 2-dr sedan	$1,947/	611/
	Ace Dlx 4-dr sedan	$2,023/	586/
	Eagle 2-dr Hradtop	$2,167/	84/
	Eagle Dlx 2-dr Hardtop	$2,222/	660/
	Eagle Custom Hardtop	$2,411/	499/
523/524	Custom 2-door sedan	/ 1,663	/ 288
525	Custom 4-door sedan	/ 1,725	/ 2,882
	Bermuda Hardtop	/ 2,709	/ 659

*Option 161 cu in, 90hp 6cyl and 226.2 cu in, 115hp, 6cyl.
**Overdrive and HydraMatic Automatic

Available optional equipment: Electric clock, Cigar lighter, Hood ornament, Locking gas cap, Radio, Turn signals, Windshield washers, Back-up lights, White side wall tires, Heater, Continental kit, Fender skirts, Oil filter, Airfoam seat cushions, Full wheel covers, Power steering, two tone paint.

Pricing, production and specifications from the Standard Catalog of American Cars by John A. Gunnell, and Encyclopedia of American Cars by Editors of Consumer Guide.

Resources and References

Encyclopedia of American Cars
By Editors of Consumer Guide

Studebaker-Complete History
By Pat Foster

Studebaker Resource
By Bob Johnson

Hudson
By Richard Langworth

Kaiser-Frazer Limited Edition
By R.M. Clark

American Independent Automakers
By Norm Mort

Rambler 1950-1969
By Pat Foster

Hemmings Classic Car
Hemmingsmotornews.com

AMC Rambler Club
www.amcrc.com

Antique Studebaker Club
www.theantiquestudebakerclub.com

Hudson-Essex-Terraplane Club
www.hetclub.org

Studebaker Drivers Club of America
www.studebakersdriversclub.com

Nash 1939-1954
By Don Narus

Standard Catalog of American Cars
By John A Gunnell

On-Line Encyclopedia
wikipedia.com

Hudson Story
By Don Butler

Kaiser-Frazer, Photo Archive
Pat Foster

Kaiser-Frazer
By Brooklands

When Sears Sold Cars-The Henry J
Conner/thepistonring.com

Book of Nashes
Hemmingsmotornews.com

Collector-Car Encyclopedia
Hemmingsmotornews.com

Antique Auto Club of America
www.aaca.org

Kaiser-Fraser Owners Club
www.kfclub.com

Nash Car Club of America
www.nashcarclub.org

Willys-Overland Jeepster club
www.jeepsterclub.com

Hudson 1939-1954
By Don Narus

Other Titles by the Author......

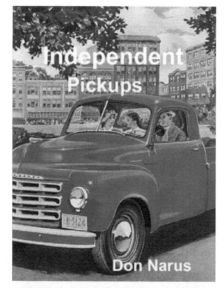

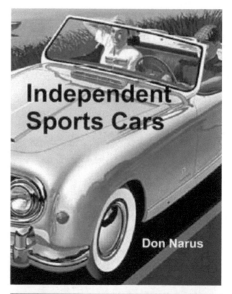

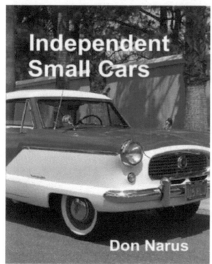

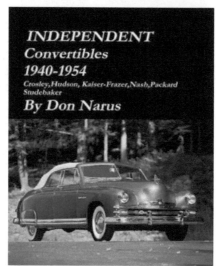

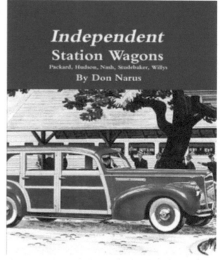

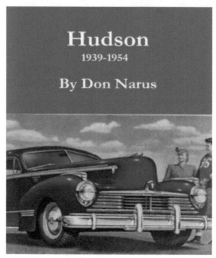

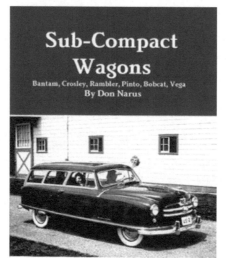

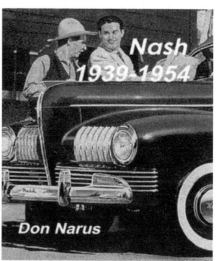

These titles by the author and many more, are available on-line from LuLu.com, or NewAlbanyBooks.com, Books4cars.com, OldMilfordPress.com. and others.

About the Author......

Don Narus is a auto historian who has chronicled American cars over the last four decades. His interest lies in the history and evolution of the American car. His books focus on the details and nuances of each model, putting you behind the wheel. The perfect primer and quick reference guide.

What others have said......

Independent Convertibles 1940-1954
Automotive historian Don Narus has a new title in his continually expanding library of auto reference books, focusing on the soft top models built by Crosley, Hudson, Kaiser-Frazer, Nash, Packard and Studebaker. The 141 page softcover is illustrated with black and white photos and advertising reprints, as well as charts listing basic statistics, list prices and production numbers. Don does a fine job placing these cars in historic context. Independent Convertibles is another great go-to reference for your automotive bookshelf, *Mark McCourt, Hemmings Classic Cars*

Independent Station Wagons 1939-1954
Don Narus has brought readers an excellent pictorial history of the station wagon produced by the independents: Packard, Hudson, Nash, Studebaker and Willys, covering the years 1939-1954. Narus has brought hobbyists many fine reference books over the years and this one continues that tradition.
Antinque Automobile, Kim Gardner

Independent Sports Cars
Independent Sports Cars delivers what its title promises. Post war sports cars like AMX,Avanti, Crosley Hot Shot & Super Sport, DeLorean, Hudson Italia, Javelin, Kaiser Darrin, Nash-Healy, as well as Packard & Studebaker Hawks are featured. All illustrated with black and white vintage and contemporary images. Nine chapters take the reader from front to rear of these vehicles, as well as interiors, dashboards, engine bays and trunks. Author Don Narus accessible writing style provides interesting anecdotes together with specifications and production figures. This soft cover is worth the ride.
Michael Petti, K-F News Bulletin

Notes